Plants We Eat

Stephanie Fitzgerald

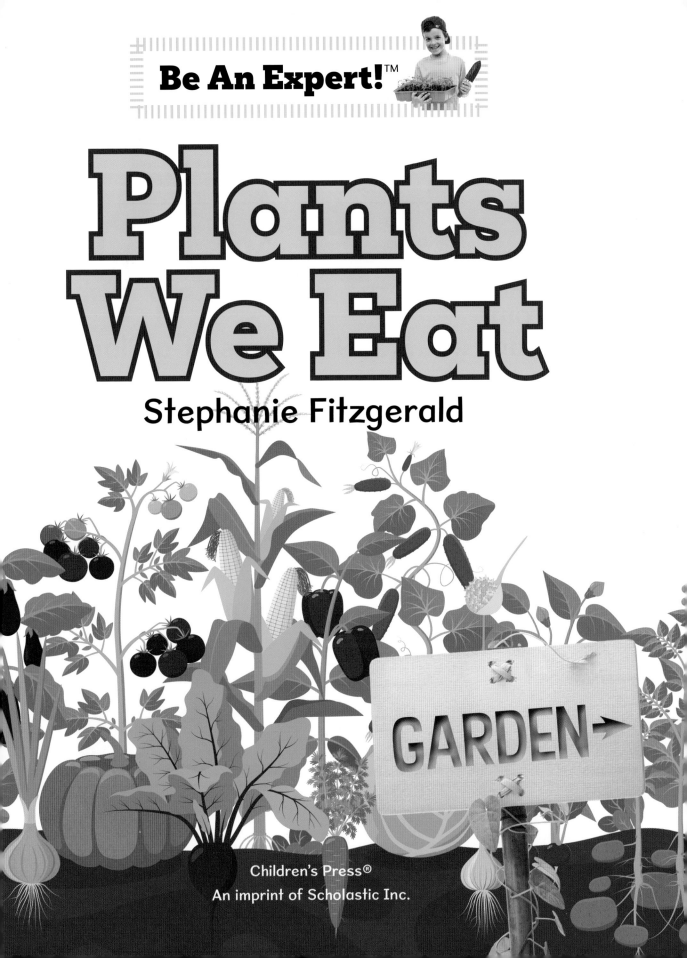

Children's Press®
An imprint of Scholastic Inc.

Contents

Know the Names

Be an expert! Get to know the different parts of plants that we eat.

Food from the Garden

Food gives us **energy** to grow and play! Many foods we eat come from plants.

watermelon

Grow Your Knowledge

Q: How are plants different from other living things?

A: Plants grow in the ground or in water. Unlike other living things, they cannot move from place to place.

corn

celery

carrots

Parts of a Plant

Plants have six main parts. We get food from all of them!

Expert Fact

Trees are plants. Their stems are covered with **bark**. Cinnamon is a **spice**. It comes from the bark of a tree.

flowers

leaves

fruits

Tomato Plant

stem

seeds

roots

Seeds

Plants grow from seeds.
Some seeds are good to eat.

Zoom In

Find these food groups in the big picture.

grains   **pods**   **beans**

rice
plant

rice

peas

pumpkin
seeds

sunflower
seeds

walnuts

pinto
beans

Roots

Roots support the plant. They take in water and **nutrients** from the soil.

sweet potatoes

carrots

radishes

beet

turnip

Stems

The stem carries water and nutrients to different parts of the plant.

chives

celery

rhubarb

Stalk is another word for *stem*. Sugar is usually made from the stalk of a sugarcane plant.

green onions

asparagus

Leaves

The leaves soak up sunlight to make food for the plant.

cabbage

red cabbage

spinach

Herbs are plants. We eat the leaves of herbs like mint, basil, and parsley.

basil

leaf lettuce

kale

chard

Boston lettuce

15

Flowers

Flowers help plants make seeds.

Zoom In

Find these flower parts in the big picture.

petal   **pistil**   **sepal**

artichokes

squash
blossoms

broccoli

16

green
cauliflower

purple
cauliflower

white
cauliflower

Fruits

The seeds for new plants are inside the fruit.

bananas

cherries

eggplant

tomatoes

pears

Grow Your Knowledge

Q: What is a stone fruit?

A: It is a fruit that has one hard pit in the center. The seeds are inside the pit. Cherries and peaches are examples of stone fruits.

watermelons

pineapples

lemons

kiwis

oranges

red apples

nectarines

green apples

grapes

peaches

corn

pumpkins

Which Part of the Plant?

They are yummy and good for you.
Thank you, plants, for so many foods

1.

2.

5.

6.

Expert Quiz

Can you name each of these foods—and which part of the plant it is? Then you are an expert! See if someone else can name them too!

3.

4.

7.

8.

Answers: 1. Celery is a stem, 2. Rice is a seed, 3. Tomatoes are fruits, 4. Basil is a leaf, 5. Walnuts are seeds, 6. Bananas are fruits, 7. Broccoli is a flower, 8. Beets are roots.

Expert Gear

Meet a horticulturist. What does she need to study and care for plants?

She needs a **trowel**.

She needs **pruners**.

She needs a **digging spade**

She needs **gloves**.

She needs a **hose**.

Glossary

bark (BAHRK): the tough covering on the stems of trees and other plants.

energy (EN-ur-jee): the ability or strength to do things without getting tired.

nutrients (NOO-tree-uhnts): things that are needed by people, animals, and plants to stay strong and healthy.

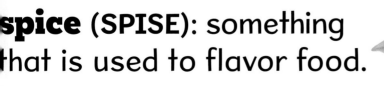

spice (SPISE): something that is used to flavor food.

Index

Library of Congress Cataloging-in-Publication Data
Names: Fitzgerald, Stephanie, author.
Title: Plants we eat/Stephanie Fitzgerald.
Other titles: Be an expert! (Scholastic Inc.)
Description: New York: Children's Press, an imprint of Scholastic Inc., [2022]. | Series: Be an expert | Includes index. | Audience: Ages 3–5. | Audience: Grades K–1. | Summary: "Some are roots. Some are fruits. Some are even flowers. What do you know about plants we eat? With this book, you can become an expert. Feel like a pro with exciting photos, expert facts, and fun challenges. Can you name a food that is a plant stem or a plant seed? Try it! Then see if you can pass the Expert Quiz!"— Provided by publisher.
Identifiers: LCCN 2021026008 (print) | LCCN 2021026009 (ebook) | ISBN 9781338797909 (library binding) | ISBN 9781338797916 (paperback) | ISBN 9781338797923 (ebk)
Subjects: LCSH: Plants, Edible—Juvenile literature.
Classification: LCC QK98.5.A1 F58 2022 (print) | LCC QK98.5.A1 (ebook) | DDC 581.6/32—dc23
LC record available at https://lccn.loc.gov/2021026008
LC ebook record available at https://lccn.loc.gov/2021026009

10 9 8 7 6 5 4 3 2 1   22 23 24 25 26

Printed in Heshan, China 62
First edition, 2022

Series produced by Spooky Cheetah Press
Design by The Design Lab, Kathleen Petelinsek
Cover design by Three Dogs Design LLC

Photos ©: 1 sign: Olivier Le Moal/Dreamstime; 5 inset top: Nagy-bagoly Ilona/Dreamstime; 5 center left: Mudplucker/Dreamstime; 7 sign: Olivier Le Moal/Dreamstime; 7 bottom tomato: Dorling Kindersley ltd/Alamy Images; 8 inset top: Wavebreakmedia/Getty Images; 9 main: John Fortunato; 12 bottom left: Barbro Bergfeldt/Dreamstime; 13 bottom left: Peter Zijlstra/Dreamstime; 16 bottom left: 4u4me/Getty Images; 18 eggplant: Alexander Iotzov/Dreamstime; 18 left: Ariel Skelley/Getty Images; 20 top left: Barbro Bergfeldt/Dreamstime; 23 top: Hanhsua/Dreamstime.

All other photos © Shutterstock.